D0177089

On the
Seashore

Schools Library Service

573534

EAST SUSSEX
SCHOOLS LIBRARY
SERVICE

573534	
Askews & Holts	May-2015
574 MIL	£4.99

Edited by Jenny Tyler and Gillian Doherty
With thanks to Dr. Margaret Rostron and Dr. John Rostron
for information about the seashore

Illustrations copyright © Erica-Jane Waters.
The right of Erica-Jane Waters to be identified as the illustrator of this Work has
been asserted by her in accordance with the Copyright Designs and Patents Act 1988.
This edition published in 2011 by Usborne Publishing Ltd, 83-85 Saffron Hill, London EC1N 8RT, England.
www.usborne.com Copyright © 2011, 2006 Usborne Publishing Ltd. The name Usborne and the devices ♔ ⊕ are Trade Marks
of Usborne Publishing Ltd. All rights reserved. No part of this publication may be reproduced, stored in a retrieval system,
or transmitted in any form or by any means, electronic, mechanical, photocopying, recording or otherwise,
without prior permission of the publisher. First published in America in 2012. UE. Printed in Dubai.

On the
Seashore

Anna Milbourne

Illustrated by Erica-Jane Waters

Designed by Laura Parker

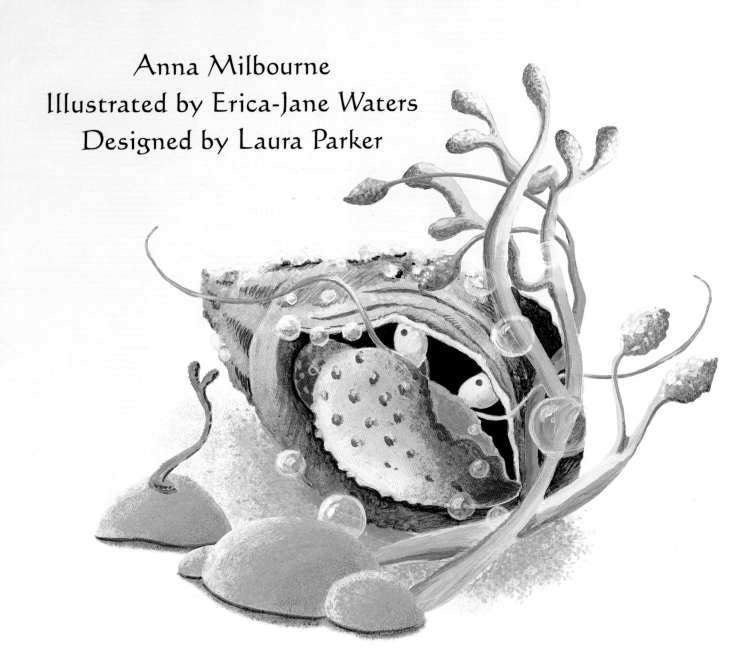

Have you ever been down to the seashore...

to look for treasures
the sea has left behind?

Sometimes, there are
trails of frilly seaweed...

and lots of dainty seashells
scattered across the beach.

And sometimes, hidden among the rocks,
there's a pool of shimmering water.

Nothing in the rock pool
seems to move at first.

But if you watch very closely,
you might see...

two shiny eyes peering
out of a small, grubby shell.

It's a little hermit crab.
He's very, very shy.

He spots a juicy mussel and
reaches out with his big, bumpy claw.

He pulls the mussel out of its shell...

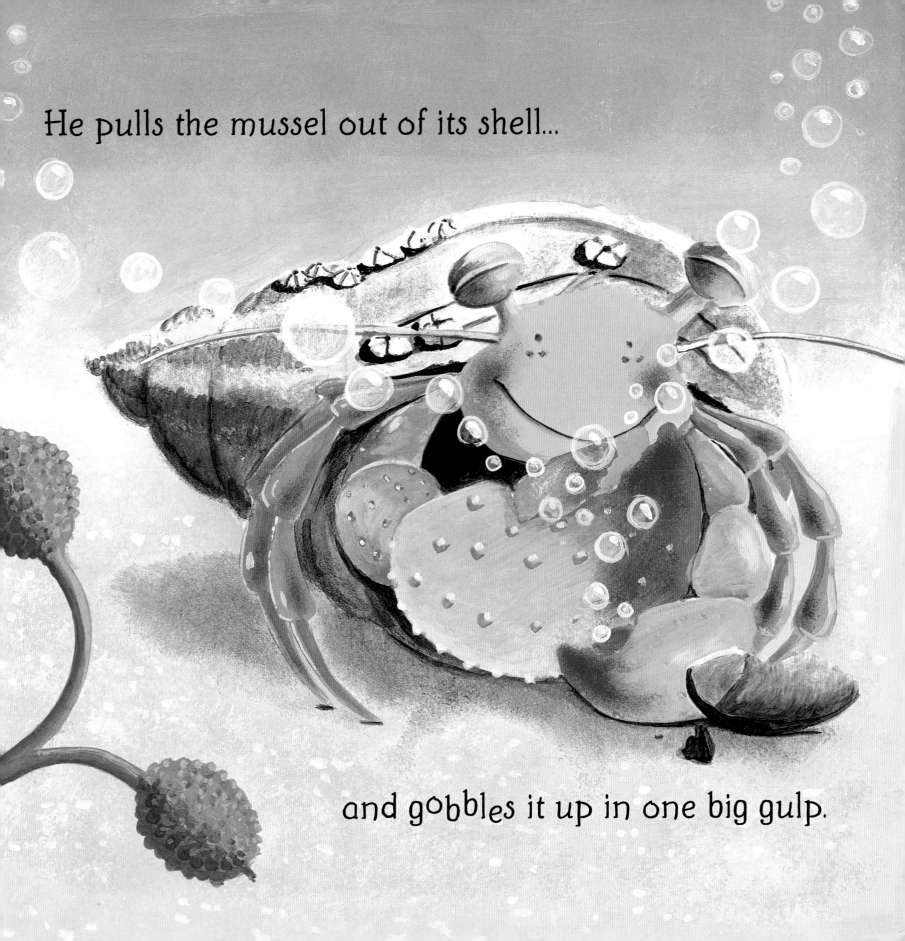

and gobbles it up in one big gulp.

The hermit crab shares the rock pool with...

a spotty fish...

three orange starfish...

...and a pretty anemone.

The anemone is sitting on a twirly shell.

The twirly shell is bigger
than the hermit crab's shell.

He feels inside it with his claw.

There's no one living there.

So he heaves himself out of his own shell,
to try the new one on.

Without his shell, the hermit crab
looks soft and rather bare.

Suddenly, a seagull
swoops out of the sky.

It wants to eat him up!

Quickly, the hermit crab
dives into the twirly shell.

The seagull tap-tap-taps hungrily on the shell.

But it can't reach the hermit crab hiding inside.

So it flies away to find its dinner somewhere else.

The little hermit crab is safe.

He drags his big, new shell across the sand.

With the pretty anemone sitting on top,
he's hard to spot at the bottom of the pool.

Soon, the gentle, lapping waves
start creeping up the seashore.

They wash away the footprints...

and swallow up the sand.

They cover the rocks,
and the rock pool disappears.

Under the waves, the spotty fish
and two tiny shrimps...

are free to swim away.

And the hermit crab clambers over the rocks...

and sets off to explore the deep, blue sea.

Maybe you'll find the hermit crab
when the sea slips away again.

Or maybe there'll be new
treasures waiting to be found.